Bill Fell

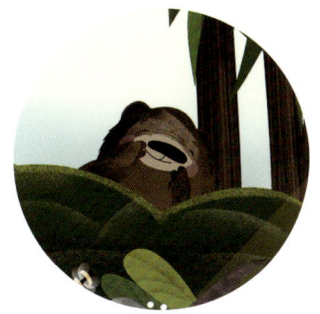

Written by
Stephen Rickard

Illustrated by
Heike Jane Zimmermann

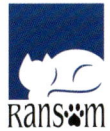

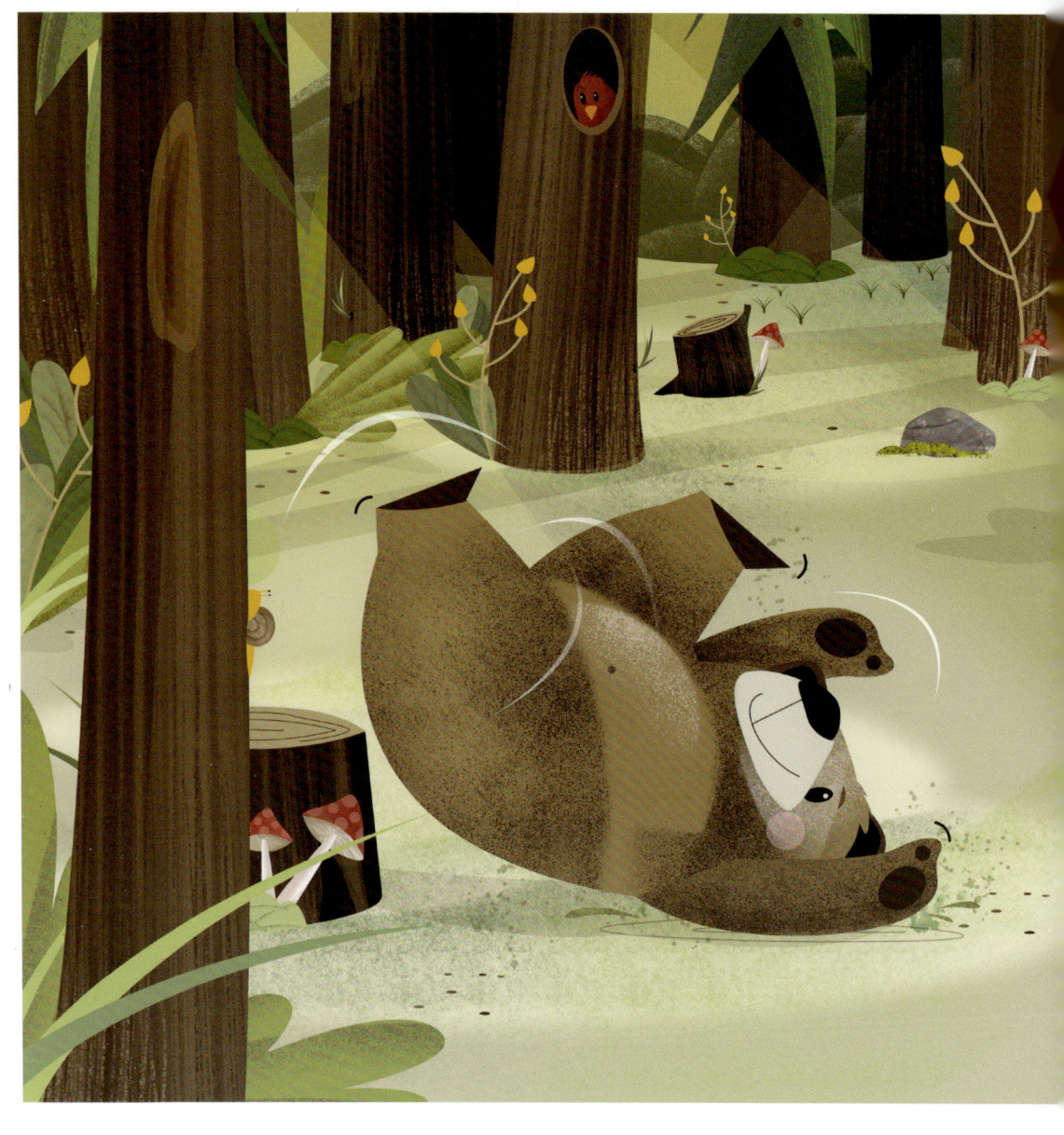

Bill fell off the log.

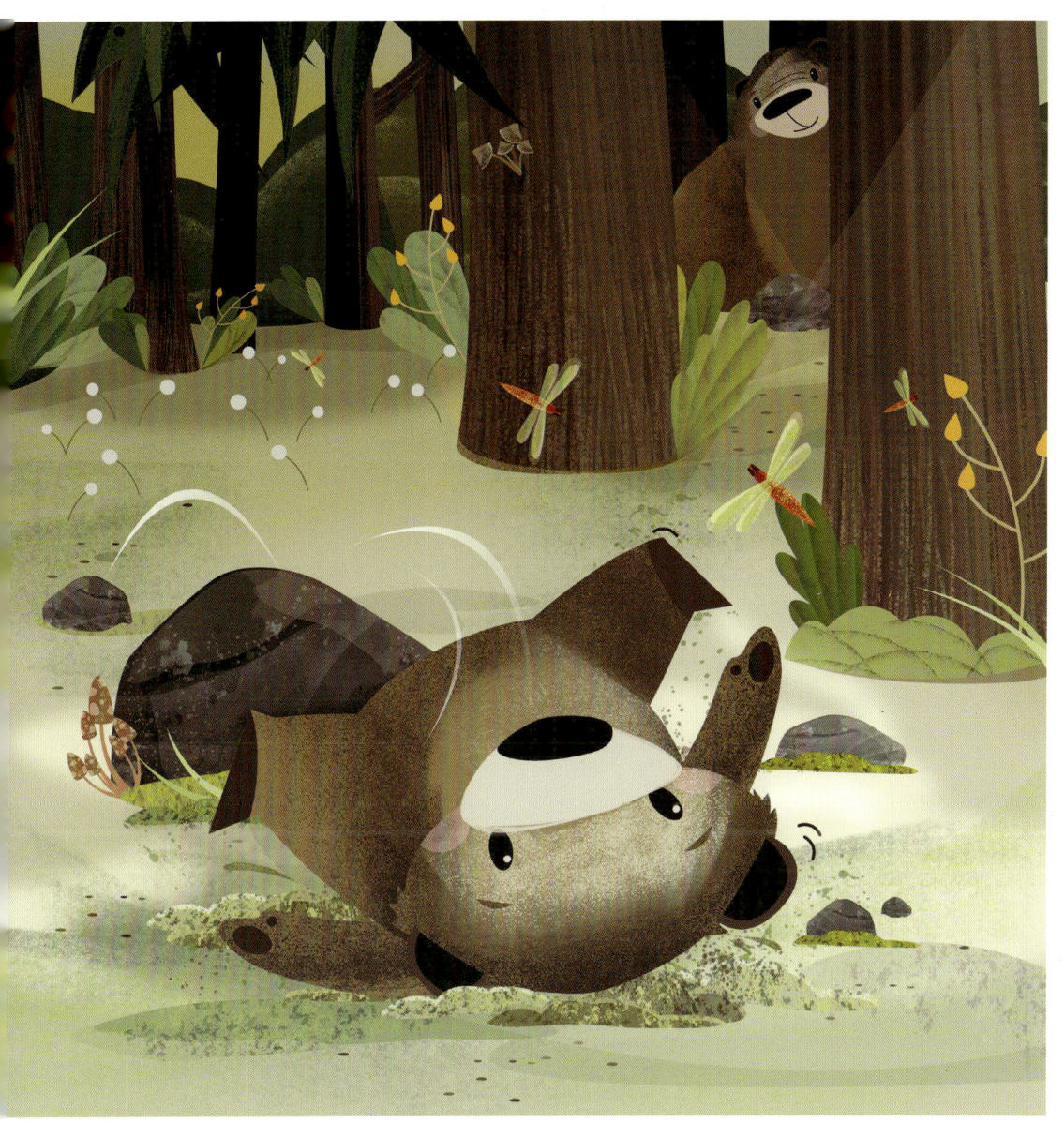

Bill fell off the rock.

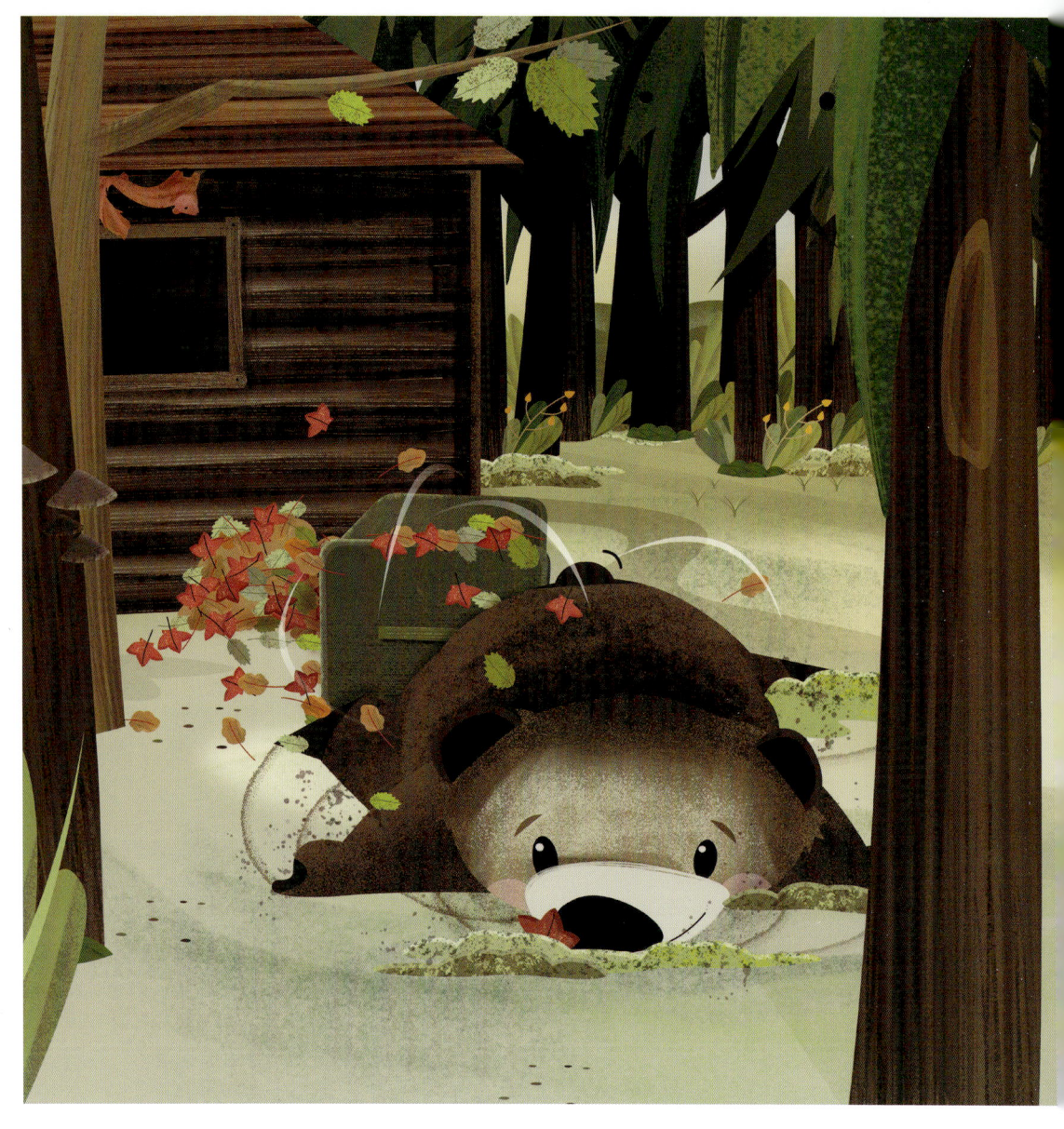

Bill fell off the bin.

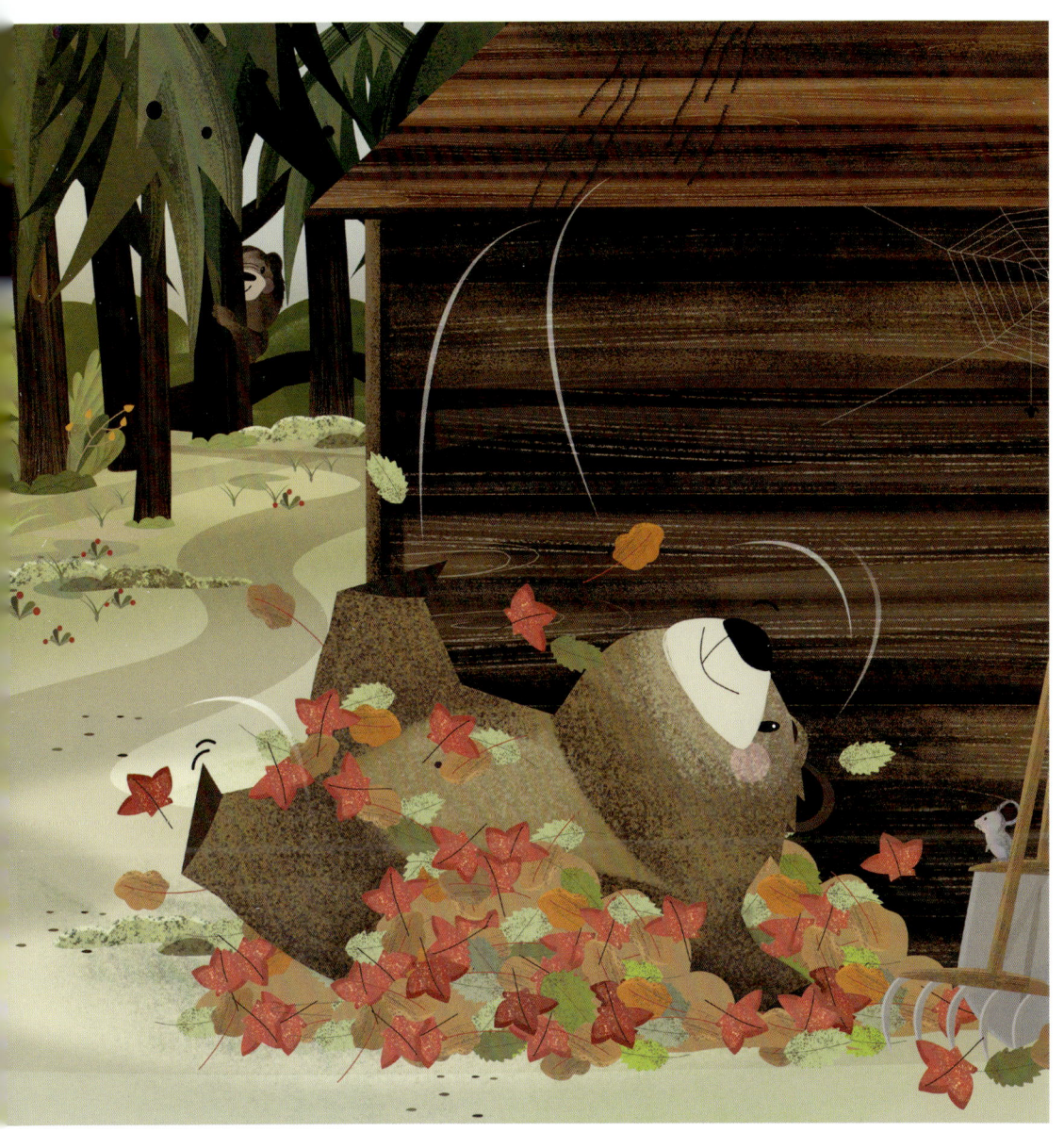

Bill fell off the hut.

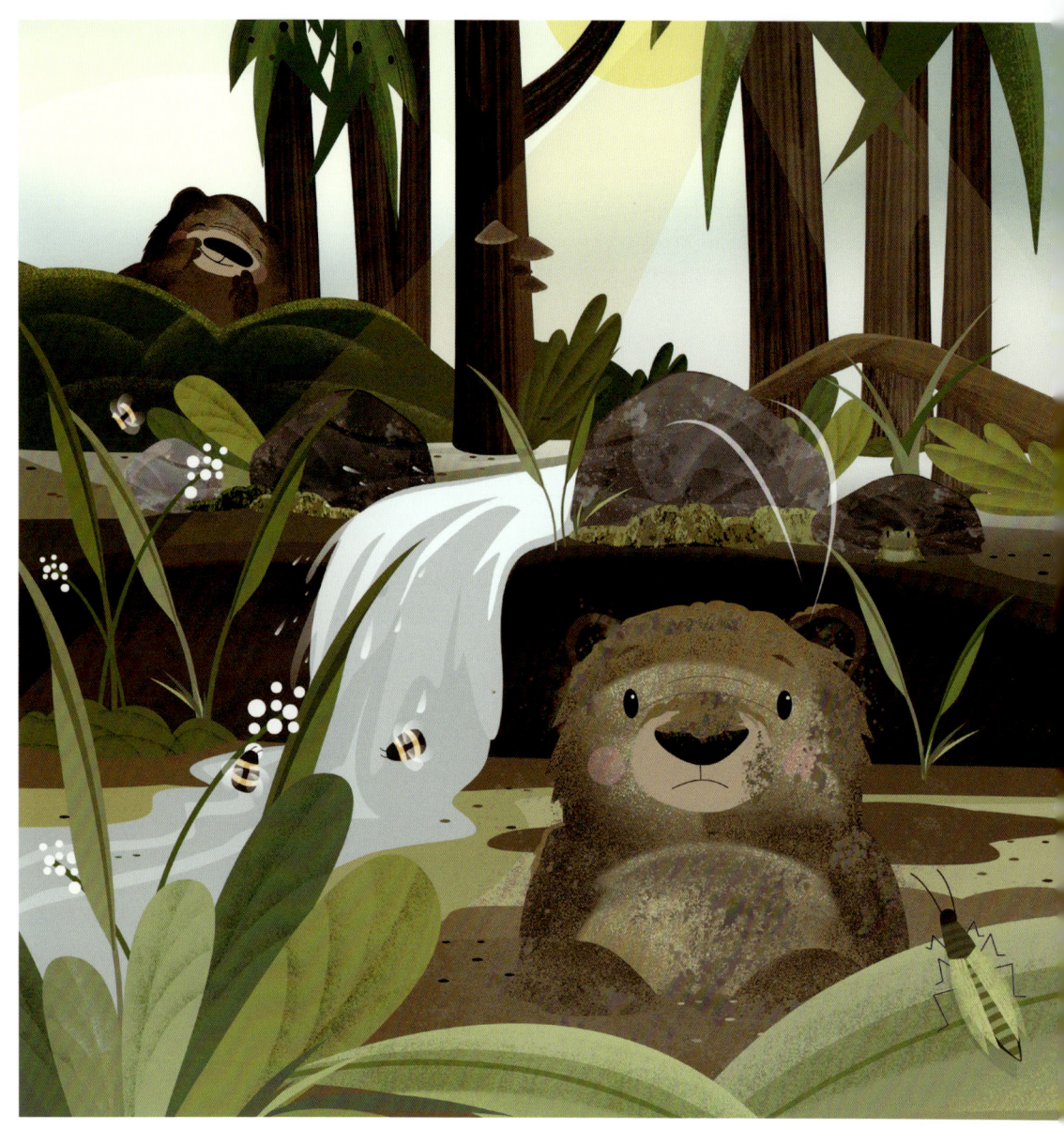

Bill fell in the mud.

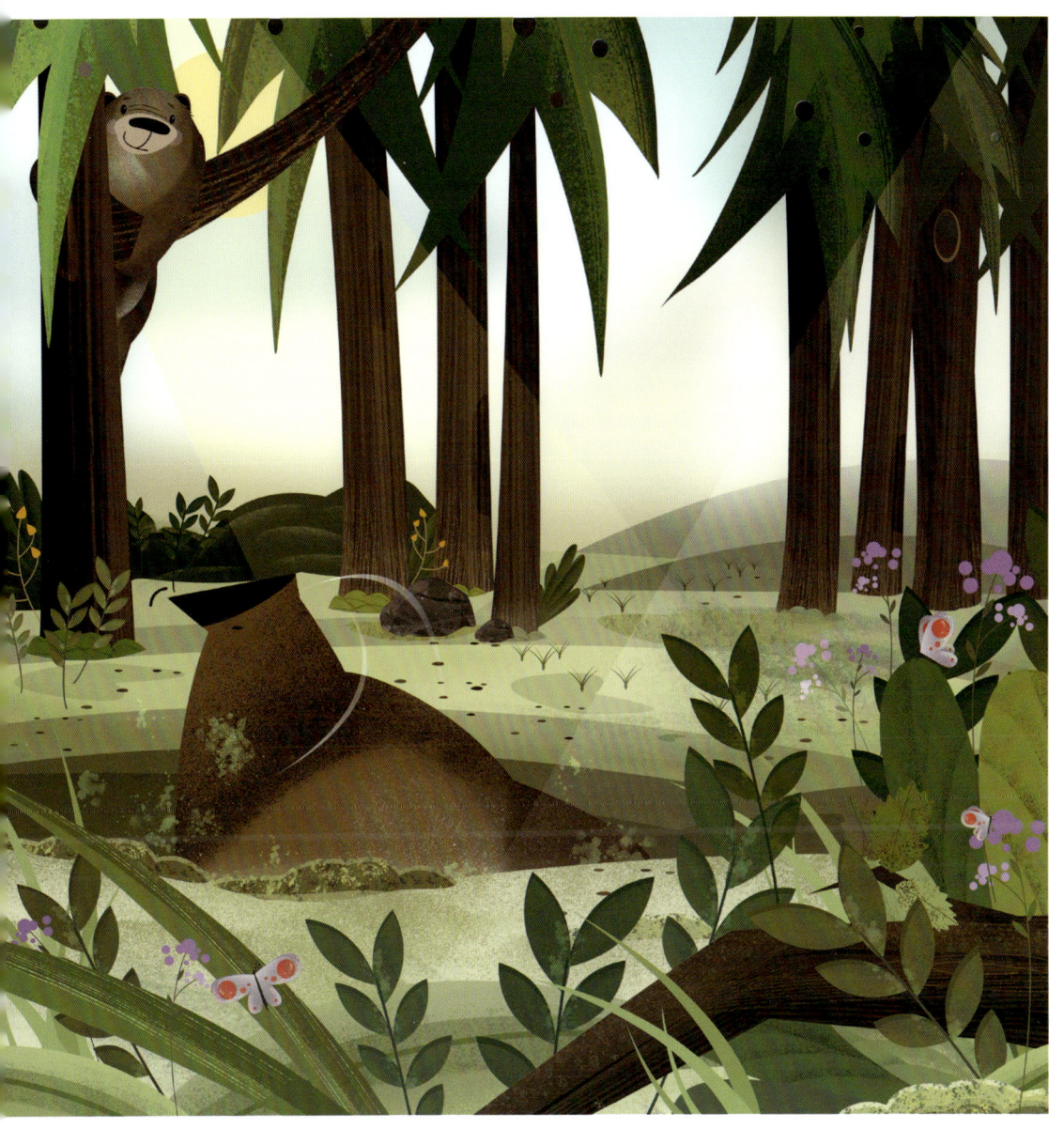

Bill fell in the dip.

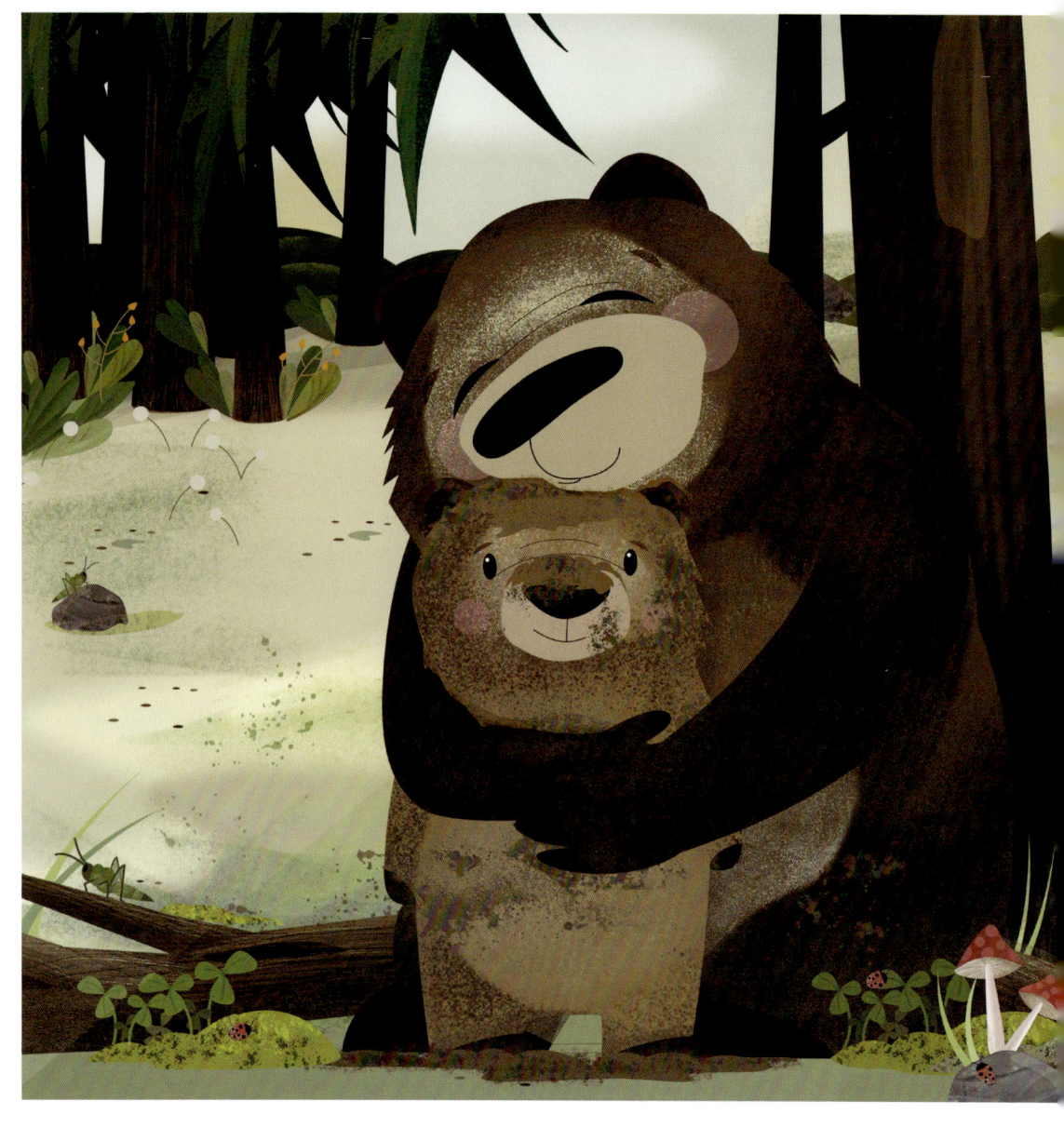

Bill got a hug and a kiss.